The Proverbs 31 Woman

The Proverbs 31 Woman

Eleanor Reid-White

Treasure House

An Imprint of

Destiny Image® Publishers, Inc.
P.O. Box 310
Shippensburg, PA 17257-0310

"For where your treasure is,
there will your heart be also." Matthew 6:21

ISBN 1-56043-612-3

For Worldwide Distribution
Printed in the U.S.A.

This book and all other Destiny Image, Revival Press and Treasure House books are available at Christian bookstores and distributors worldwide.

For a U.S. bookstore nearest you, call **1-800-722-6774**.
For more information on foreign distributors,
call **717-532-3040**.
Or reach us on the Internet: **http://www.reapernet.com**

Contents

Preface

As a minister of the gospel, I have gained a burden for the women in the body of Christ. I have spoken to many women who desire to be married but do not know what to do in order to prepare for it.

I, like many women of God, want to be married and I've often wondered why it has taken me so long to meet the right person. However, I have submitted myself to God and I refuse to marry anyone other than the man He has chosen for me.

As I sought the Lord in preparation for marriage, His wisdom directed me to begin by studying Proverbs 31:10-31. In doing so, I found that the scriptures that I studied were not only beneficial for women preparing for marriage, but they edify **all** women of God who are moving towards holiness and preparing for ministry.

As I studied, I learned that God would not allow part of the body to prosper and leave the other parts lacking. It is imperative for those of us who have gained knowledge and wisdom to share it, in its various forms, with the other parts of the body. Therefore, I am submitting this revelation of God's word to you so that we, as women and men of God, can know and walk in truth.

Although *The Proverbs 31 Woman* focuses on preparing women for marriage, motherhood and ministry, I believe that men can benefit from this revelation on the character of a Proverbs 31 woman. It is important for us to keep in mind that the husband's diligence in the Lord effects the consistency of a Proverbs 31 wife.

Men will be spiritually edified by reading this book, because it:

- gives them insight into what God desires for them
- will encourage them to edify, exhort, and esteem their wives as virtuous women of God
- will exhort them to search the Word for knowledge and to gain wisdom on what God requires of them in a marriage and for Christ-like living.

Finally, this book will illustrate to married couples the characteristics that a marriage should possess and the significant steps to take to have a marriage the way God intended it to be.

Hopefully, *The Proverbs 31 Woman* will inspire you to study further the areas of marriage, ministry, and godly lifestyle. Beyond the first chapter, there are few stories. However, there is instruction and guidance through the revelation. I have provided space so that each reader can note the application of the study to her or his life.

The general emphasis of the work is individual preparation through right relationship with God. Each person must be whole before two can become one.

I pray that the revelation I received on the Proverbs 31 woman will be a blessing to you, as you study these verses in preparation for marriage, for ministry, and for life.

Chapter 1

Preparation

In December of 1991, I attended a friend's wedding and had the opportunity to speak at length to some of my covenant sisters in the Lord. We talked about the Proverbs 31 woman. I planned to get married later the next year, but things did not work out as they should have in order for a marriage to take place. I became discouraged because I believed that I was ready for a marital relationship.

Before my friend's wedding, the Lord dealt with me concerning marriage and my relationship, through three distinct dreams. In the first dream I was involved in an endurance race, that I skillfully planned to win. However, part way through the course, I realized that I had not looked at the course map. Although I had planned to pass the leader in the final phases of the race, I fell far behind everyone because both the leader and I did not know the way.

In the second dream, I was adrift on a river with several other people, mostly women. We all had our own wooden rafts for support. However, when the waters became rough my raft began to break into pieces and before long, I just had a few boards to hold onto.

The third dream was the most poignant. It had a medieval setting. I was in a tower with my boyfriend, who happened to be the court jester. I was determined to marry him. We were truly in love with each other. He was the silliest man you had ever seen, but I decided to settle for him anyway. I even tried to get up under him physically to submit. But he was so lowly that I couldn't do it.

Attached to the tower was a wide wall that extended into an ocean and on the other side of the ocean stood a large castle, which was connected to the wall. The castle was resting on a small island that seemed lost in the middle of the water. My mother kept urging me to marry the prince of the castle, but I adamantly refused.

I looked out of the tower window and I saw the prince walking slowly and majestically toward the tower with his arms stretched out to me. He was smiling peacefully. Seeing him come to me made me hold onto the jester even tighter. After the prince arrived in the tower, my mother (again) began to urge me to go with him. I kept refusing but the prince just stood patiently smiling at me.

Finally, the jester convinced me to go with the prince and sadly let me go. Reluctantly, I went. The prince picked me up in his arms and began to carry me slowly across the wall to the castle. As we traveled across the wall I took a long hard look at him. He was handsome and stately, confident and strong. I quickly concluded that this wasn't such a bad move after all.

When we arrived at the castle, he brought me to the top floor and set me in my room. From the room's window I looked back at the tower and I noticed that the tower, not the castle, was sitting in the middle of the ocean. I became quickly convinced that God had someone better for me than who I could choose for myself.

Other Witnesses

Besides the three dreams, I received another witness in a letter from a friend. She included a scripture that the Lord led her to give to me.

Many daughters have done virtuously, but thou excellest them all. Prov. 31:29

For two weeks before my friend's wedding, the Holy Spirit kept telling me to study Matthew 25:3:

The foolish ones took their lamps but did not take any oil with them. Matt. 25:3 (NIV)

I studied this for many days, although I was unsure why.

The day before my friend's wedding, I had the opportunity to speak with his father. This man was literally filled with the Word and had committed many scriptures to memory. Under the unction of the Holy Ghost, he would lace his conversation with scripture that would always speak to what was going on in the hearer's life. Of all the scriptures he mentioned in our conversation, one in particular stuck with me.

Sow to yourselves in righteousness, reap in mercy; break up your fallow ground: for it is time to seek the Lord, till He come and rain righteousness upon you. Hos. 10:12

Revelation

Finally, as I spoke to my covenant sisters that night, it all came together. God sees me as a Proverbs 31 woman, just as He saw Gideon as a mighty warrior before he went up before the Midianites (Judges 6-7). Yet, there was something I had to do to live up to God's vision of me...obediently PREPARE.

All three dreams illustrated that I was not prepared. Matthew 25:3 explicitly stated it. When I realized that I was not ready, I was no longer anxious about getting married. So, I began to focus on what God required for readiness, and Hosea 10:12 began to show me how to prepare.

Preparation for marriage is like preparing fallow or unplowed ground for a seed. Before one sows seed, the ground has to be tilled, turning over and removing the weeds and rocks of untruth and rhetoric. The dirt can then be supplemented with manure to increase the ground quality so that we're left with a rich soil ready for seed. In application, we need to make sure our acquaintances speak words of life not gossip to us and around us. We should seek to be where the Word of God is going forth.

Now we can sow good seed into this freshly prepared ground, and it will take root and produce because it has been sown in good ground (Matt. 13:3-9). The seed of preparation that I planned to sow would prepare me not only for marriage, but for ministry both inside and outside the home.

An important thing that I realized about my preparation was that I would be prepared according to the Word and not according to man's definition of preparedness.

Proverbs 31 was a good starting point. For this woman is not only a good wife, but she exemplifies the character of a godly woman.

Favour is deceitful, and beauty is vain; but a woman that feareth the Lord, she shall be praised. Prov. 31:30

One of this woman's key characteristics is **discipline**. When we begin to practice discipline and self-control, we will have less trouble submitting to God. By learning to submit ourselves to God, we will have no trouble submitting to our husbands.

Getting Ready

As we prepare, we must keep in mind that the men we marry must also prepare themselves for marriage according to the Word. We (women) should know the characteristics of a prepared man, so that we will not be easily fooled by any man claiming us as his "wife in the name of the Lord."

A few scriptures that will give women examples of prepared and unprepared men are: Genesis 1-3, Ephesians 5-6, I Peter 3, Colossians 3, and Titus 2. Some relevant character studies are Abraham and Sarah, Genesis 18-22; and Nabal and Abigail, I Samuel 25.

Married and unmarried women must also study parental responsibilities (alone or with a spouse or fiancé). Many scriptures that contain parental advice are in the previously mentioned scriptures.

When God calls us out of a life of sin and into His kingdom, He intends for us to take on the same character as His son Jesus Christ. After we have done this, He considers us as firstborns who will receive the inheritance of our Father.

> *For whom He did foreknow, He also did predestinate to be conformed to the image of His Son, that He might be the firstborn among many brethren.*
> Rom. 8:29

Our behavior, which builds our character, affects every area of our life. When we take on the character of Christ, as this woman does, we will become established in all things—from our physical body, finances, and careers to our relationships.

Notes

Chapter 2

Substance

Verse 10

A wife of noble character who can find? She is worth far more than rubies. (NIV)

Who can find a virtuous woman? for her price is far above rubies. (KJV)

Key Words

Virtuous	= honorable, high principled, modest, strong, of substance
Noble	= renowned, excellent
Character	= behavior, reputation
Ruby	= a deep red precious stone

A wife of excellent behavior and reputation is more valuable than precious stones. God chooses His words with purpose. Precious stones have value because of their rarity or appearance. The ruby's value lies in its distinct deep red color.

In God's infinite wisdom, he placed verse 10 as the first of the 21 verses, so that we could see the need to establish ourselves in Him before entering a marital relationship or moving out into ministry.

The Proverbs 31 woman is worth more than rubies because this woman is filled with substance (virtue, honor). She is knowledgeable and has obtained wisdom from God. Her beauty runs deep below the surface and permeates every organ of her body. Her spirit is regenerated and is in line with the Holy Ghost. Her mind has been transformed by the Word of God. Even her emotions exemplify her beauty, because she feels deeply the afflictions of others and makes a point of doing something for them. She is neither superficial nor flighty. She is "deep."

This woman is wise and carries herself and her conversation in wisdom and esteem. She expresses love and the fruits of the spirit in all that she says and does. She walks in love, in joy, in peace, in patience, in kindness, in goodness, in faithfulness, in gentleness, and in self-control (Gal. 5:22-23).

This woman of high moral character may not be apparent to those who walk in the flesh or observe her in the natural. To see her godly qualities, we must look beyond her flesh and see her spirit (see I Cor. 2:14).

...look not on his countenance, or on the height of his stature; because I have refused him: for the Lord seeth not as man seeth; for man looketh on the outward appearance, but the Lord looketh on the heart. I Sam. 16:7

Setting the Right Priorities

Man is inspired by and wants to develop what he sees, however, God takes a different approach to development. God works from the inside out. We are spirit beings living in a vessel of flesh.

So God's priority is to get the believer together and walking in line with His perfect will. Once she is together, her spirit will impact how she takes care of that which is outside.

We establish our character through our relationship with God and exemplify it through our confidence in Him. Without having a spirit yielded to obedience and submission toward God, we cannot achieve and walk in the attributes of a godly woman.

Remember the old expression, "She's a diamond in the rough"? Well, many of us are still "rubies in the rough." We are in the process of being refined and shaped into the jewels God desires for us to be.

The Proverbs 31 Woman Is of Excellent Character

Notes

Chapter 3

Trustworthiness

Verse 11

Her husband has full confidence in her and lacks nothing of value. (NIV)

The heart of her husband doth safely trust in her, so that he shall have no need of spoil. (KJV)

Key Words

Heart	=	feelings, mind, will (soul)
Safe	=	reliable, dependable, sound
Trust	=	confident, sure, worry-free
Confidence	=	trust
Spoil	=	stolen goods, loot, plunder
Value	=	worth, benefit, significance

As women, our primary responsibility is to God and then to our families. The man should be the main vessel through which God provides for the household. This does not suggest that he should make the most money or have the largest salary, but the family's financial obligations should be dependent primarily upon his income. The wife's income should be supplementary at most. If the family is dependent on two incomes and they remain dependent upon them, even when the husband can meet the needs of his family, then the family is living beyond their means.

In turn, our husbands should trust us with household affairs. We ought to be prudent in spending, not foolishly wasting the family's resources.

As wives, we should work diligently in our homes, leaving no room for worries (example: a wife overspending the budget without consulting her spouse) when our husbands return.

Needless to say, part of preparation is practice. As single women, we should first practice good home management in our own homes. We won't have a "good housekeeping anointing" dropped on us the moment we say, "I do." Through practice and diligence things become learned behavior and are internalized.

Although practice is critical in obtaining the God-like characteristics we eventually want to have, practicing the wrong thing can cause us to be out of God's will. As Christians, God lets us know that we cannot practice sin, but righteousness.

In the which ye also walked some time, when ye lived in them.

But now ye also put off all these; anger, wrath, malice, blasphemy, filthy communication out of your mouth.

Lie not one to another, seeing that ye have put off the old man with his deeds;

And have put on the new man, which is renewed in knowledge after the image of Him that created him. Col. 3:7-10

I constantly try to do those things that God would have me to do, and I am sharpening myself in the areas where I may be weak. Therefore, when God says that it's time to get involved with what He has planned for me, I will be ready.

A Body Fitly Joined Together

The husband is the head of the household, but he has delegated a significant portion of the managerial responsibilities to his wife. He is not free from all household responsibility, but he doesn't have to manage it directly.

Although many people don't include God in their affairs, a husband and wife should seek God and come to a consensus about what responsibilities they will share around the house. The Word lets us know that if we would seek Him in all that we do, He will give us direction.

In all thy ways acknowledge Him and He shall direct thy paths. Prov. 3:6

The man must first submit to God, so that his wife can submit to him. Many women are afraid to submit because they and some men confuse it with obedience.

Obedience is taking and carrying out the orders of another without question. Submission is, upon conferring with another, taking their suggestions over ours and carrying them out.

God doesn't make us do anything. We decide to follow Him and to obey Him. And, when women make the decision to get married, we acknowledge that we will submit to our husbands. On the other hand, by making the same commitment, the man implies that he is submitted to God and he will take on the responsibilities of the headship position.

The head sees, hears, speaks, and represents the whole body. The head, in seeing, hearing, and speaking, protects the body from oncoming danger by directing it away from harm. It also nourishes and nurtures the body so that it can function according to God's will; and it motivates the body to operate effectively in the vision established for that body.

Wives, submit yourselves unto your own husbands, as unto the Lord.

For the husband is the head of the wife, even as Christ is the head of the church: and He is the savior of the body.

Therefore as the church is subject unto Christ, so let the wives be to their own husbands in every thing.

Husbands, love your wives, even as Christ also loved the church, and gave Himself for it;

That He might sanctify and cleanse it with the washing of water by the word,

That He might present it to himself a glorious church, not having spot, or wrinkle, or any such thing; but that it should be holy and without blemish.

So ought men to love their wives as their own bodies. He that loveth his wife loveth himself.

For no man ever yet hated his own flesh; but nourisheth and cherisheth it, even as the Lord the church:

For we are members of His body, of His flesh, and of His bones.

For this cause shall a man leave his father and mother, and shall be joined unto his wife, and they two shall be one flesh.

This is a great mystery: but I speak concerning Christ and the church.

Nevertheless let every one of you in particular so love his wife even as himself; and the wife see that she reverence her husband. Eph. 5:22-33

The body speaks to the head to let it know what's going on inside. When the body hurts, the head hurts as well and it makes haste to apply a salve to ease the pain. The body also lets the head know what does and does not work in caring for it internally (certain medicines don't work for everybody). When the head hurts, the body that supports it hurts also and it shifts the balance of things in the body to fight the root of that head pain and bring comfort.

Dealing With the Imperfect

If a saved and submitted woman of God has an unsaved or unsubmitted husband, she has an obligation to pray for him and walk uprightly before him. In any marriage there is a certain degree of submission that is required. However, submission to an unsubmitted husband stops at the point where his requests are out of line with the Word of God. And, God will give you this wisdom to know how to deal with an imperfect situation.

> *Likewise, ye wives, be in subjection to your own husbands; that, if any obey not the word, they also may without the word be won by the conversation of the wives; while they behold your chaste conversation coupled with fear.* I Pet. 3:1-2

God takes care of His own. No man nor any weapon formed by man can prosper against God's people. God will fight every battle for us. When we let Him fight the battles, we gain the victory and cannot be faulted because we did not physically engage in the battles. Whatever God instructs you to do or say will not give the appearance of competition between you and God and your husband. But it should result in your safety.

For the eyes of the Lord are over the righteous, and his ears are open unto their prayers: but the face of the Lord is against them that do evil.

And who is he that will harm you, if ye be followers of that which is good? I Pet. 3:12-13

For every battle we should seek wise counsel. This is part of your pastors' purpose. They, too, having submitted themselves to God, should be able to instruct you according to the Word of God.

Where no counsel is, the people fall: but in the multitude of counsellors there is safety. Prov. 11:14

Trust

In dealing with some personal situations, God gave me a deeper revelation of I Peter 3:1-7. First, we, as women, need to be careful about how we handle a man's love for us. Second, in submitting to that man of God, we must be careful not to burden him with foolishness.

Trust is a foundation for any relationship and one must be careful not to betray the trust between a husband and wife. This trust extends beyond household affairs. When someone loves you they are sharing and entrusting their emotions to you. That is why we can only get hurt by those we love.

Likewise, when we don't allow the Spirit to move through us like He would desire to or don't make the changes in our behavior that we need to in order for Him to dwell in us, we grieve Him (Eph. 4:20-32).

A sacred trust exists between a husband and wife that must be upheld within and beyond the boundaries of the relationship. Nothing should cause division, but they should allow the Holy Ghost to unite them and bring oneness.

Sometimes men in love will do almost anything to make their wives happy, including things that are unrighteous. When we spend excessive time daydreaming and constantly mentioning the list of things we want to have, but can't afford at the moment, we place a burden on our mates to get those things for us quickly.

When your husband becomes overburdened and pressured to supply your soulish desires, the enemy then has an opportunity to attack him. The devil will begin to show him how he can get those things, though the family budget can't manage it right now. The enemy will remind him of past acquaintances who can hook him up with a short-term, quick-money deal. He will also show him how certain bills can go lacking or dedicated savings can be used. Yes, he will even tell him that he can skip paying his tithes for a few months, and make it up later if he wants to.

However, when the husband and wife begin to renew their minds, the enemy can give them ideas and suggestions, but they will begin to reject them and cast them out by the Word of God. (See Colossians 1:21-23.)

(For the weapons of our warfare are not carnal, but mighty through God to the pulling down of strong holds;)

Casting down imaginations, and every high thing that exalteth itself against the knowledge of God, and bringing into captivity every thought to the obedience of Christ. II Cor. 10:4-5

Everything our flesh or our minds want, God does not necessarily want for us. For instance, we may want new furniture, however, God may not want us to get it yet. Check with God first. If God says you can have it, then wait for His instruction. He may or may not want you to tell your husband what He has told you concerning getting or not getting the furniture. Now, God will reveal it to your husband whether you tell him or not. So if God does want you to tell him, then you will provide a confirmation to him concerning that thing.

Controlling Our Tongues

However, trust goes even beyond desires. God may not want you to tell your husband about every bad dream, what someone said about someone else, or how you stumped your toe on the door. God wants us to use wisdom in what we say to our husbands, so that we can be careful not to burden them with things that are not of good report or things that the Lord hasn't led us to tell them. Sometimes we want to talk about some of everything. But we can't let our desires override the will of God. Instead, we are to tell God and cast all our cares on Him. Sometimes we will need to pray through on our own.

Let your moderation be known unto all men. The Lord is at hand.

Be careful for nothing; but in every thing by prayer and supplication with thanksgiving let your requests be made known unto God.

And the peace of God, which passeth all understanding, shall keep your hearts and minds through Christ Jesus. Phil. 4:5-7

We don't always know what God is working into and out of our mates. That's why we always have to hear what God is saying to us about how to deal with them at any given point. We have to control the words that we say, so that our husbands will feel good about themselves and the righteous efforts they make to meet the family's needs and desires.

...A quarrelsome wife is like a constant dripping. Prov. 19:13 (NIV)

We all know how annoying a constant dripping can be. Some of the synonyms for quarrelsome are:

> whining
> complaining
> self-willed
> froward
> deceptive ("catty")
> difficult
> disagreeable
> angry
> ill-tempered

Guarding our tongues is important to any successful relationship, especially the marital one. Death and life are in the power of the tongue.

Death and life are in the power of the tongue: and they that love it shall eat the fruit thereof.

Whoso findeth a wife findeth a good thing, and obtaineth favour of the Lord. Prov. 18:21-22

When we begin to kill our relationships with our words, we are in essence killing ourselves. We and our husbands have become one flesh. Therefore, if the relationship ended, the pain and the grief would be great. Because, separation is like tearing out your own flesh.

Therefore shall a man leave his father and his mother, and shall cleave unto his wife: and they shall be one flesh. Gen. 2:24

When we guard our tongues and focus on speaking words of comfort, exhortation, and edification, our husbands will have no need of spoil. They won't feel compelled to steal to meet foolish desires. They don't have to think about stealing because we haven't squandered the finances away. They can trust us because we are the help meet and support we should be.

The Proverbs 31 Woman Is Trustworthy and Supportive

NOTES

Chapter 4

True Friendship

Verse 12

She brings him good, not harm all the days of her life. (NIV)

She will do him good and not evil all the days of her life. (KJV)

Key Words

Good	= upright, honorable, loyal
Evil	= meanness, indecency, scandal

Often, women are said to be creatures of emotion, more sensitive and more expressive than men. People also say that we confide in others often, especially other women, our deepest thoughts.

As God dealt with me concerning this verse, the sanctity and oneness of the marriage relationship became the overriding theme of the revelation.

Wives, as well as husbands, must be that friend and confidant even when things are not at their best in or out of the home. We must speak words to comfort, edify, and exhort him 'all the days of his life'. This requires a special sensitivity to his needs. There is a time to speak and a time to lay low. When we do speak, there is a time to say certain things and a time to let other things go completely. We should always be a vehicle of peace and comfort.

Besides being a vehicle of peace and comfort, we must also open ourselves to receive any kindness our mates want to shower upon us. We may think that this is an easy thing to do, but some of us have been hurt so often and so deeply that we even have trouble opening up to receive of God. Because so many of us are accustomed to giving of ourselves and not receiving from others, we do not know how to or are uncomfortable receiving love when it is returned.

We find it hard to receive the love of God and His benefits fully, because of fear. Despite satan's attempts to separate us from God's love with fear, God's all powerful love prevails once we let go of our thoughts and trust in His word. Therefore, it is important to cast down every thought that is not of God, which tries to replace the truth of God.

And you, that were sometime alienated and enemies in your mind by wicked works, yet now hath He reconciled

In the body of His flesh through death, to present you holy and unblameable and unreproveable in His sight:

If ye continue in the faith grounded and settled, and be not moved away from the hope of the gospel, which ye have heard, and which was preached to every creature which is under heaven; whereof I Paul am made a minister. Col. 1:21-23

Many men have difficulty expressing their feelings. So, they need to feel comfortable enough with us to share whatever feelings and expressions of love they can give. We, in return, should not expect love to come in any particular form (e.g., flowers daily, presents weekly, going out to dinner all the time), but we should understand our husbands well enough to know when and through what means he expresses love toward us.

In public, we should never say things contrary to our husbands decisions or opinions. Whatever we say should agree with what he says. Otherwise, we shouldn't say anything at all. When we speak of our husbands, we should only speak words of praise. We should keep words of praise in our mouths, even when we talk to our relatives about our mates. Since relatives are the most likely to be sensitive to our experiences, they usually get defensive if they feel we are being mistreated. This does not mean that we are dishonest about our situations or that we hide the truth, but we must be careful of what we say and to whom.

We should strive to do everything (caring for ourselves, family, home, and associating with others) in honor and do nothing to shame our husbands.

The Proverbs 31 Woman Is Honorable

NOTES

Chapter 5

Ministry

Verse 13

She selects wool and flax and works with eager hands. (NIV)

She seeketh wool, and flax, and worketh willingly with her hands. (KJV)

Key Words

Wool	=	fleece, soft hair of sheep or other animals (e.g. goats)
Flax	=	a beautiful plant from which linen is made
Eager	=	fervent, willing, enthusiastic
Hands	=	the hollow of the palm, power or strength

This woman has established herself as part of the ministry. Only priests wore wool and flax (a type of linen). In fact, there was a law forbidding others to wear wool and linen. Highly valued by the Hebrews, wool represented purity. This godly woman took the time to select fine materials, and then used her talent to create garments worn by the ministers of that day.

We should also note that she worked eagerly (or with a strong desire) and in a timely completion. Because of her relationship with God, she wanted to contribute to the ministry in any way that she could, so she found her place in the ministry and occupied it faithfully.

Spinning or weaving was a female industry of honor. Although women may have been limited to tasks such as the making of garments, they did those tasks with dignity and pride. Perhaps because they recognized that every role within the body was important and honorable.

Verily I say unto you, Wheresoever this gospel shall be preached in the whole world, there shall also this, that this woman hath done, be told for a memorial of her. Matt. 26:13

We need to consider our role or roles in the ministry prayerfully and carry them out with honor and devotion, remembering that no role is too small or insignificant. Every part must work and then work together in order for the body to function properly.

The Proverbs 31 Woman Is an Active Part of the Body of Christ

NOTES

Chapter 6

Self Education

Verse 14

She is like the merchant ships, bringing her food from afar. (NIV)

She is like the merchants' ships; she bringeth her food from afar. (KJV)

Key Words

Merchant	= trader, exporter, dealer
Ships	= carriers, transports
Food	= something that nourishes, a solid taken in allowing a person to grow.

Ships are sent out on missions. They go out and come back having done what they were sent out to do. Merchant ships leave port for foreign lands in search of precious finds that cannot be gotten in their cities. The merchants bring back rare and beautiful treasures that the people in their land would like and would be willing to pay a premium for.

Part of our development, as women of God, is learning. We should take time to become educated on various topics of interest to ourselves and to our households. We can attend seminars, take classes, or attend events in which we have an opportunity to learn more about those things that impact the lives of our families and those we minister to. We can then bring that knowledge home and share it with others who may not have the time or resources to get it for themselves.

It is important that we, both men and women of God, are storehouses of knowledge. For without it, we would perish. It is satan's job to deceive us by feeding us lies. Deception is his number one weapon against us. With it, he tricks us into taking our eyes off God and putting them on our circumstances. By coming against our mind with pictures that lie, he attempts to destroy our faith in God's word. Once we believe what satan says, we have taken the bait, because belief leads to action.

Since we believe in God, then we should take action according to what God has said. We must not truly believe in God if we don't do what He says. If we are not moving according to what God has said, then we are moving according to what the devil has said.

So many of us then end up in trouble because we have been lured away from God's protection by satan's lies. When we take ourselves from under God's protection we are open to the enemy's attacks.

The only way we can avoid deception is to know the truth. When we know the truth for ourselves, we are then able to rightly divide truth from untruth. When we don't know, confusion grows and we are open to believe anything. As women of God we are responsible for knowing both spiritual and natural things so that our families will not be led astray in any matter.

The Proverbs 31 Woman Is Informed

NOTES

Chapter 7

Responsibility

Verse 15

She gets up while it is still dark; she provides food for her family and portions for her servant girls. (NIV)

She riseth also while it is yet night, and giveth meat to her household, and a portion to her maidens. (KJV)

Key Words

Food	= something that nourishes, a solid taken in allowing a person to grow
Night	= sinking of the day, a dark season, adversity
Household	= family, house
Portion	= necessary measure

Godly women are responsible. Being responsible for something other than ourselves implies that we can no longer be selfish in our thinking and actions. We cannot be lazy or slothful, but we must make full use of the time God has allotted us. No longer sinners, our thoughts are now toward what is best for our households and those to whom we minister.

This means that we will often make personal sacrifices to ensure that our households and ministries are attended to daily. If that means we have to get up a little earlier, we do it because our primary responsibility is to God and not ourselves.

Furthermore, we cannot skimp and do things half-heartedly. God has shown us perfect faithfulness in all love. We, then, must be faithful in our doing, and do with all our hearts.

We have to organize so that everything that needs to be done within the day gets done. In all that we do, we must be diligent and not complain, but rejoice because we have been blessed with the ability to do these things.

The Proverbs 31 Woman Is Responsible

NOTES

Chapter 8

Entrepreneurship

Verse 16

She considers a field and buys it; out of her earnings she plants a vineyard. (NIV)

She considereth a field, and buyeth it: with the fruit of her hands she planteth a vineyard. (KJV)

Key Words

Consider	= value, recognize
Field	= an open and unfenced area that has to be watched day and night
Vineyard	= a highly valued field of vines the fruit of which can be used for many things.

Many believe a woman's only place is in the home. However, God created man to have dominion over the earth and to work the land. Since God saw that it was not good for man to be alone, he created a help meet or the woman for him. God created woman to help man have dominion and to work the land (Gen. 2:25). We see in Proverbs 31:16 further indication of a woman's responsibility to work and what areas she should direct her earnings toward.

The Proverbs 31 woman is a shrewd entrepreneur. Why is she an entrepreneur? If we look back at the last five verses we see that she is a woman of awesome responsibility. Did you ever wonder why most women are good organizers and planners? We need the flexibility that entrepreneurship provides in order to manage and fulfill our responsibilities.

Take a minute or two to think about the many talents you have. Write them down. There are a broad array of talents in the body of Christ such that we do not need to go outside the body to get them. There are handy talents such as catering, tailoring, and constructing, as well as, service oriented talents such as planning, organizing, and counseling. God gave all of us a measure of talents. So, there is a business in you somewhere (Matt. 25:14-30).

And unto one he gave five talents, to another two, and to another one; to every man according to his several ability; and straightway took his journey. Matt. 25:15

Many people don't believe they can run a business, because not everyone has the ability to run a large enterprise. Often, people equate business with large operations. But we have to know how God wants us to employ our talents in business. Some businesses can be run out of our own homes with only one person as an employee. Others will require office or manufacturing space with many employees. Still some talents are most profitable within the context of someone else's business.

Nonetheless, we have before us the answer to the question that has been plaguing the women of the 80's and 90's, 'How to balance family and career?'

As an entrepreneur, we gain the freedom of decision and greater flexibility. Although we may have to work more than eight hours a day, we can decide based on our customer's needs which hours to work and which to spend taking care of other responsibilities. If child care is an issue, we can employ or give room to someone else with that talent in or close to our place of business so that we can spend more time with our children during the day. The list of benefits far outweigh any negatives.

And that ye study to be quiet, and to do your own business, and to work with your own hands, as we commanded you. I Thess. 4:11

In God's Time

None of this means that we should quit our jobs tomorrow to strike out on our own. We need to seek God for the timing of the moves we need to make. God will ensure that we have received all of the value necessary from working for other companies. We can learn a lot about business by taking note of how other companies function. Ask God for wisdom about what to read, who to ask questions of, and what events to attend.

We should use the spirit of discernment to understand what constitutes good and bad business practices. It may take one, five, or ten years for us to gain knowledge from outside work experiences. Patience and diligence will prepare us to move out into our own businesses.

The success of our ventures is dependent on our obedience to God today and every day going forward. God will bring us into the place of blessing that He has for us as we stay submitted to Him (Josh. 1). Once He brings us to that place, we have to stay submitted to prosper in that place.

Priorities

However, we must remember that none of these works, be they in business or in ministry, precede God or our households in priority. All our responsibilities must be prayerfully balanced. Women who are out of balance become frustrated because they have to spend too much time on a job and not enough time with their families. Many working women want to have children but often they don't because they can't envision having children and working.

On the other side, many homemakers carry talents that they don't believe can be used because of their obligation to their families. God has given us talents not to hold onto but to use for His purpose. Whatever our business options are, the ones that are right will ensure we have the needed flexibility to care for our homes.

The Purpose for Increase

Let's look now at how the Proverbs 31 woman uses her earnings. She first looks around to find a field and then she buys it. But to buy that field she had to have money and enough of it. Many scriptures call for us to be prudent and stewardly.

Houses and wealth are inherited from parents, but a prudent wife is from the Lord. Prov. 19:14 (NIV)

A prudent man foreseeth the evil, and hideth himself; but the simple pass on, and are punished. Prov. 27:12

He said therefore, A certain nobleman went into a far country to receive for himself a kingdom, and to return.

And he called his ten servants, and delivered them ten pounds, and said unto them, Occupy till I come. Luke 19:12-13

Someone once explained it to me this way. "All the money we earn belongs to God since He has provided and we belong to Him" (Luke 19:11-27). Therefore we need to consider prayerfully what to do with our earnings after we have given our tithes, offerings, and alms. Most certainly our bills must be paid on time so that we do not defraud others and dishonor God. God will direct us on the amount we should save from each pay period.

There are a number of reasons to save. One reason God wants us to save is so that we can obtain those things that we asked Him for and He said we could have. When we obey God in our finances, we will see how He perfectly moves those things that we want in our path once we can afford them.

Yes, God will make us to know how much of our earnings can be used for miscellaneous things. I contend that we still need to pray over miscellaneous spending. There must be something gained from our every purchase. God is not a God of waste and wantonness. For example, it's okay to eat out as long as there is a good reason. Fellowship and rest are two good reasons. There is no way that you can't be a financial winner by allowing God to control your finances.

Being Faithful

The Proverbs 31 woman uses her earnings to plant a vineyard. Vineyards often are symbolically used throughout the Bible. Grape vines have a few interesting characteristics.

The cultivation of grape vines is a very involved process. It takes almost a year and a half of cutting, growing, and pruning before vines can then be replanted in a vineyard. To protect the fruit it must be picked by hand and growers must consistently prune and manage the vine's growth, since they have a tendency to grow wildly.

Another characteristic is that the vines produce an abundance of fruit. Each vine produces between 15 and 20 pounds of grapes. The grapes themselves are probably one of the best used fruits. Every part of the grape can be used. The uses range from pure fruit and juice to inks and mayonnaise.

As saints of God, we are to invest our resources wisely. Our investments should be with a long term view, and in things that will produce an abundant harvest and can be fully used to produce more wealth to meet our ongoing needs.

The principle of sowing and reaping holds true in every area of our lives. If we sow good seeds today, the result will be good fruit, from the profits of which we can sow more seed. Therefore, we will continually prosper.

Even beyond finances, we should use our gifts and talents to serve others.

As every man hath received the gift, even so minister the same one to another, as good stewards of the manifold grace of God. I Pet. 4:10

As we bless others we will be blessed (II Cor. 9:6-15).

But this I say, He which soweth sparingly shall reap also sparingly; and he which soweth bountifully shall reap also bountifully. II Cor. 9:6

The Proverbs 31 Woman Is a Good Steward

NOTES

Chapter 9

Ability

Verse 17

She sets about her work vigorously; her arms are strong for her tasks. (NIV)

She girdeth her loins with strength, and strengtheneth her arms. (KJV)

Key Words

Gird	=	surround, to prepare oneself for action
Vigorously	=	energetically, eagerly, purposefully
Loins	=	lower region of the back considered the seat of strength
Task	=	responsibility, business

The Proverbs 31 woman is diligent in those things that she has charge over. She devotes herself to her responsibilities, be it ministry or family. She remains focused and puts forth an earnest effort in all that she does. She is efficient, effective, able, and capable because God has equipped her for her tasks. She is a help meet.

God gives us a mind or desire to do His will. As we renew our minds through the Word, we begin to think like Christ. Having taken on Christ's Spirit, we begin to act like Him. Additionally, God has allowed us to go through particular circumstances, so that certain desires and talents would become a part of us. He then puts us into positions where our talents and experiences can be used with purpose. Now that we have established the character and responsibilities of a virtuous woman, verse 17 speaks to our willingness and ability to carry out all our obligations.

We are to be diligent in all our works. If we are not faithful and diligent over our tasks, we will have done little to nothing. God will not put on us any more than we can bear. Therefore, God has made us capable and has given us the strength to do all that He requires of us. Likewise then, He will not require us to do more than we can do.

After a long time the lord of those servants cometh, and reckoneth with them.

And so he that had received five talents came and brought other five talents, saying, Lord, thou deliveredst unto me five talents: behold, I have gained beside them five talents more.

His lord said unto him, Well done, thou good and faithful servant: thou hast been faithful over a few things, I will make thee ruler over many things: enter thou into the joy of thy lord.

He also that had received two talents came and said, Lord, thou deliveredst unto me two talents: behold, I have gained two other talents beside them.

His lord said unto him, Well done, good and faithful servant; thou hast been faithful over a few things, I will make thee ruler over many things: enter thou into the joy of thy lord. Matt. 25:19-23

We, as women, have many responsibilities, but they should not overwhelm us. If we find ourselves dragging to get things done, we are probably doing too much or not taking the time to organize ourselves properly. Never forget that God has strengthened us, not to be work horses or to be driven, but to cultivate and to advance the Kingdom.

The Proverbs 31 Woman Is Capable

NOTES

Chapter 10

Quality

Verse 18

She sees that her trading is profitable, and her lamp does not go out at night. (NIV)

She perceiveth that her merchandise is good: her candle goeth not out by night. (KJV)

Key Words

Trade	=	commerce, enterprise, business
Profitable	=	lucrative, useful, beneficial
Lamp	=	torch, a device that gives light when burned

We should be women of value and we are to look for value in whatever we are involved in or buy. We should devote ourselves toward things that will be valuable to our families and others. We should focus our thoughts on how we can improve the things that we have charge over. We need to use the wisdom of God in our efforts and work untiringly, even through the night if necessary.

We need to perform our jobs and talents to the best of our ability. If the tasks are done, but not done well, they will not profit others or ourselves to the extent God intended for them to prosper.

So then, if we have to get up early (verse 15) to do all we must do (verse 16), knowing that we have been given the ability to do these things (verse 17), and if we have to stay up a little later at night to complete our tasks (verse 18), we ought to do it. Why? Because we are working for God not for man (I Cor. 3:5-11; Eph. 6:7).

Who then is Paul, and who is Apollos, but ministers by whom ye believed, even as the Lord gave to every man?

I have planted, Apollos watered; but God gave the increase.

So then neither is he that planteth any thing, neither he that watereth; but God that giveth the increase.

Now he that planteth and he that watereth are one: and every man shall receive his own reward according to his own labour.

For we are labourers together with God: ye are God's husbandry, ye are God's building.

According to the grace of God which is given unto me, as a wise masterbuilder, I have laid the foundation, and another buildeth thereon. But let every man take heed how he buildeth thereupon.

For other foundation can no man lay than that is laid, which is Jesus Christ. I Cor. 3:5-11

With good will doing service, as to the Lord, and not to men. Eph. 6:7

Working is a form of worship. We worship not only verbally, but with our actions as well (Col. 1:9-14).

And we pray this in order that you may live a life worthy of the Lord and may please him in every way: bearing fruit in every good work, growing in the knowledge of God. Col. 1:10 (NIV)

The Proverbs 31 Woman Is Faithful

NOTES

Chapter 11

Diligence

Verse 19

In her hand she holds the distaff and grasps the spindle with her fingers. (NIV)

She layeth her hands to the spindle, and her hands hold the distaff. (KJV)

Key Words

Distaff	= a staff used to hold wound flax and wool for spinning
Spindle	= a thin rod used in spinning

The Proverbs 31 woman can keep everything under control and yet keep working. She is self-controlled, alert, and disciplined.

The distaff and spindle are parts of the weaving machine. The spindle holds the thread and the distaff is used to wind the thread. These devices the Proverbs 31 woman uses to control the spinning process. Notice that she controls the raw products or inputs to the final product.

God gives us seeds to work with, whether they are talents, gifts, or ideas.

Now he that ministereth seed to the sower both minister bread for your food, and multiply your seed sown and increase the fruits of your righteousness. II Cor. 9:10

It is up to us to sow or employ those seeds into good and fertile ground. Once we have sown and watered, God will give the increase. But we first must sow our seeds. We must work diligently.

We are responsible for being good stewards over what God has given us. As diligent workers, we must employ ourselves fully in all that we do.

The soul of the sluggard desireth, and hath nothing: but the soul of the diligent shall be made fat. Prov. 13:4

Nothing should be done halfheartedly but rather with our whole hearts as unto Christ.

The Proverbs 31 Woman Is Diligent

NOTES

Chapter 12

Compassion

Verse 20

She opens her arms to the poor and extends her hands to the needy. (NIV)

She stretcheth out her hand to the poor; yea, she reacheth forth her hands to the needy. (KJV)

Key Words

Open	= accessible, introduce
Reach	= touch, approach
Needy	= underprivileged, destitute

Part of our character as women of God is compassion and sincerity. We are to bless those in need and make sacrifices for the good of others when we can. We should have no problem giving because we realize that all our blessings come from God who will continue to supply all our needs. Not only that, but God will bless us for our liberality.

He that hath pity upon the poor lendeth unto the Lord; and that which he hath given will He pay him again. Prov. 19:17

Our ministries extend far beyond our own homes and churches. Our places of work and the paths to work are outlets for ministry. It is because we are faithful over our other responsibilities that we have enough to share and the time to spend with others.

The Proverbs 31 Woman Is Compassionate

NOTES

Chapter 13

Wisdom

Verse 21

*When it snows, she has no fear for her household;
for all of them are clothed in scarlet.* (NIV)

*She is not afraid of the snow for her household: for
all her household are clothed with scarlet.* (KJV)

Key Word

Scarlet = very bright red, royal red cloth used
in the Old Testament as a sign or
symbol

Scarlet in this scripture represents a covering or
safety. Rahab tied a scarlet cord in her window so that
when the Israelites came against Jericho, she and her
household would not be harmed (Josh. 2:18-21).

King Lemuel was being taught here that his wife should walk in wisdom and use that wisdom to take care of her own. Abigail, the wife of Nabal, was such a wise woman that in the end she married a king (I Sam. 25).

In the face of danger or hardship, we should not have to worry because we have ensured the well-being of our families by walking in righteousness. We should always be aware of what is going on around us in both the spiritual and in the natural. We have to be in tune with the Holy Ghost so that we can obtain wisdom from God on every matter. We only need to ask Him for it.

If any of you lack wisdom, let him ask of God, that giveth to all men liberally, and upbraideth not; and it shall be given him. James 1:5

When we act upon God's wisdom we ensure the safety of our households. God will always direct us away from danger and shield us from evil.

I will say of the Lord, He is my refuge and my fortress: my God; in Him will I trust.

Surely He shall deliver thee from the snare of the fowler, and from the noisome pestilence.

He shall cover thee with His feathers, and under His wings shalt thou trust: His truth shall be thy shield and buckler. Ps. 91:2-4

The Proverbs 31 Woman Is Wise

NOTES

Chapter 14

Self-Respect and Confidence

Verse 22

She makes coverings for her bed; she is clothed in fine linen and purple. (NIV)

She maketh herself coverings of tapestry; her clothing is silk and purple. (KJV)

Key Words

Silk	= Fine, soft fiber
Purple	= crimson clothing worn as an emblem of royalty

This woman keeps herself at her best. She never looks unseemly but always puts her best foot forward.

She keeps her home clean, comfortable, and present-able. This woman adds to and enhances whatever she receives. She takes the time to make the home comfort-able for her family, especially for her husband. She adds a personal touch to her home and makes it a place her family desires to be.

The clothes that she wears symbolize the charac-teristics of a dignified woman. Her linen clothing rep-resents respect and dignity, and the color purple represents her royalty.

Besides performing various tasks, we must take good care of ourselves. We don't only represent our families, but we represent God. Whenever we step out of the house, or spend a significant amount of time in the house, we need to look our best. Think about it. How can we encourage others to follow Christ when we look pitiful? You might say looks don't matter, but it's the in-side that counts. That is not true. Everything counts and what's on the inside dictates how we care for what's on the outside. The sinner is caught up in what he or she sees. So they will first judge us by what they see.

Personal hygiene is very important. Both cleanli-ness and neatness are required. We represent God, the King of Kings. We can't let our outward appearance be-come a stumbling block to our ministries.

If we need to exercise, to gain strength, then we need to be faithful in working out. If we're overweight, then we need to go on a Holy Ghost directed diet and exercise program. Our hair should always be in place, and our clothing should be pressed and cleaned. We don't have to wear expensive things or pay the highest prices for services, but we do need to be tidy with what we do have.

Our bodies are the vehicles we use to do those things which God has purposed for us. If we destroy our bodies or fail to take proper care of them, we inhibit the spirit from working through us to the fullest extent.

Flee fornication. Every sin that a man doeth is without the body; but he that committeth fornication sinneth against his own body.

What? know ye not that your body is the temple of the Holy Ghost which is in you, which ye have of God, and ye are not your own?

For ye are bought with a price: therefore glorify God in your body, and in your spirit, which are God's. I Cor. 6:18-20

We know that beauty doesn't come from our outward appearance.

Whose adorning let it not be that outward adorning of plaiting the hair, and of wearing of gold, or of putting on of apparel;

But let it be the hidden man of the heart, in that which is not corruptible, even the ornament of a meek and quiet spirit, which is in the sight of God of great price. I Pet. 3:3-4

However, how we think and who we think we are is reflected in our outward appearances. Even stress, worry, and low self-esteem are reflected on the outside, eventually. That is why it is so important that we know who we are and walk in that confidence.

But ye are a chosen generation, a royal priesthood, an holy nation, a peculiar people; that ye should show forth the praises of Him who hath called you out of darkness into His marvellous light. I Pet. 2:9

Single women should take special care to practice and continue in these things. Remember that Proverbs 31 is a queen telling her son, the king, what to look for in a wife. A woman fit for a king carries and dresses herself in such a way to attract a king.

The Proverbs 31 Woman Is Regal

NOTES

Chapter 15

Waiting in God

Verse 23

Her husband is respected at the city gate, where he takes his seat among the elders of the land. (NIV)

Her husband is known in the gates, when he sitteth among the elders of the land. (KJV)

Key Words

Known	=	recognized, accepted, received
Gate	=	a structure controlling passage through an opening, possession of the gate symbolizes power and wealth
Elders	=	older persons with authority in the community

Our husbands will gain respect when our character lines up with the Word. We will bring honor on our households by being faithful unto God in all our responsibilities. Our husbands gain respect from others because others recognize that, as the head, he **must** be submitted to God and thus walking uprightly himself, in order for his wife and family to prosper.

Only submitted men of God are apt heads of households (Eph. 5:25-33; Col. 3:19; I Tim. 3:1-7). It is so important that we as women wait for God to send our husbands to us. As we wait, we should prepare, and we wait so that we will be prepared when God's chosen time has come.

Don't settle! God will give us the desires of our hearts. We should ask for what we want and wait for God to answer us. Notice that I did **not** say ask for whom we want. We need to put our faith in what God has told us we can have and stand on **His** word. God will assure that our desires line up with what's best for us, if we submit ourselves to Him (Phil. 4:4-7).

Let your moderation be known unto all men. The Lord is at hand.

Be careful for nothing; but in every thing by prayer and supplication with thanksgiving let your requests be made known unto God.

And the peace of God, which passeth all understanding, shall keep your hearts and minds through Christ Jesus. Phil. 4:5-7

Don't worry! Your physical organs won't stop working if you don't get married tomorrow. Remember Sarah and Hannah. Don't lose your faith! In the kingdom of God there is no shortage of good men. What you see and hear does not always represent an accurate picture.

God is preparing the best for His best. If a man has not submitted himself to God and his life does not line up with the word, then he is not ready for anyone. Marriage is God's institution created for people that are submitted to Him. (Remember Adam and Eve before the fall.)

Exercising Patience

Anyone who is not submitted to God should remain single and out of closely knit girlfriend and boyfriend relationships. We have to bond with Him first (Matt. 6:25-34).

But seek ye first the kingdom of God, and his righteousness; and all these things shall be added unto you. Matt. 6:33

By building a relationship with God first, we will avoid much of the heartache and destruction associated with wrong relationships.

If someone else runs to get that unsubmitted man and marries him, then he was not for us. No one's wisdom or plan can prevail against God's. Secondly, the two that married before their time will have much to work through to get their relationship in line with the Word.

God showed me this following illustration about marriage relationships. He is the master potter. When

He puts a man and a woman together, it is like taking a piece of clay shaped into a handle and smoothing it into the jar it was made to fit. That smoothing is the initial getting to know one another after marriage. The handle and the jar have to give a little in order for the fit to be perfect.

However, when the jar and the handle decide that they want to be matched with something they were not made for, God will still honor that decision. But now, instead of a smoothing, there is a breaking of both the jar and the handle. God has to change both pieces in order for them to fit. Breaking and rebuilding takes a lot longer and is more painful than smoothing.

That is why some women and men may go through more than 20 rocky years waiting for their mates to get saved and their marriages to work out. Some people, because they never learned to submit to God, have never seen the marriage become what it could have been.

We are all part of the same puzzle. It may seem like a lot of pieces fit together. But in fact, each piece only fits perfectly with certain other pieces. We have to wait for God to match us with the proper pieces.

Transition to Marriage

Marriage is not a reward for welldoing. It is just another step toward Kingdom building. Therefore we should not expect to be perfect when we get married. There is some spiritual growth that can only take place after we are married, but we must live up to the level of maturity we have already attained (Phil. 3:12-16).

Nevertheless, whereto we have already attained, let us walk by the same rule, let us mind the same thing. Phil. 3:16

When we submit, God will confirm within us whether a man who approaches us is the one He has chosen. Not everyone who claims us as wife will be speaking a word inspired by the Holy Ghost. We are more valuable than rare jewels. Men will come from everywhere to find us; therefore, we must stay submitted to God so that we will know His voice.

When we unite with our mates, there will be a multiplication of the two lives. The woman's walk with God does not go away and neither does the man's. However, both of their walks become greatly enhanced and the two paths become one united path. The united path is greater than if you simply added the two separate paths.

The woman doesn't stop thinking for herself nor does the man, but the woman, because she knows how to submit to God, lacks trouble submitting to the man. The man, because he is submitted to God, knows how to care for and build up a submitted wife properly. Without both people submitting to God, the proper growth and maturity as well as prosperity cannot occur.

The Proverbs 31 Woman Is Submitted to God

NOTES

Chapter 16

Ministry and Enterprise

Verse 24

She makes linen garments and sells them, and supplies the merchants with sashes. (NIV)

She maketh fine linen, and selleth it; and delivereth girdles unto the merchant. (KJV)

Key Words

Girdle	= a belt for the waist
Sash	= an ornamental band worn around the waist or over the shoulder

Our talents should be used not only to earn income but to support the ministry. God has a purpose for each talent He has given us.

As every man hath received the gift, even so minister the same one to another, as good stewards of the manifold grace of God. I Pet. 4:10

Additionally, He gives us talents that we would enjoy using. The ultimate purpose for our talents is to advance the Kingdom of God. We use our talents in businesses to earn income, because money is what buys the things that we need. Income is a means to an end not an end unto itself. When God meets our needs, it will be easier for us to focus our attention on Him and minister as He would have us to minister.

Behold that which I have seen: it is good and comely for one to eat and to drink, and to enjoy the good of all his labour that he taketh under the sun all the days of his life, which God giveth him: for it is his portion.

Every man also to whom God hath given riches and wealth, and hath given him power to eat thereof, and to take his portion, and to rejoice in his labour; this is the gift of God.

For he shall not much remember the days of his life; because God answereth him in the joy of his heart. Eccles. 5:18-20

The businesses we start, be they restaurants, law firms, or beauty salons should be outlets for the ministry in one way or another. They should be founded on the Word, and their rules and guidelines should be rooted in the Word. We will meet sinners through our businesses that will be drawn by the success that they see. When they ask us how we could attain such success, we can give our testimony of God's grace toward us and our obedience to Him.

These sinners were predestined to be ministered to by us. So if we haven't done what we were supposed to do with what God gave us, we will be found guilty. Remember the man with the one talent that buried it. Because the world is so driven by financial success, these sinners will be open to be ministered to by us because they respect us for the prosperity that they see (I Thess. 4:11-12).

So that your daily life may win the respect of outsiders and so that you will not be dependent on anybody. I Thess. 4:12 (NIV)

God has placed all the necessary talents and skills for everything in the body of Christ. If everyone were to rise and use their gifts, we would find that the body is self-sufficient. It is not God's desire for us to have to run to the world to get anything. The wealth of the wicked is stored up for the just.

To the man who pleases him, God gives wisdom, knowledge and happiness, but to the sinner he gives the task of gathering and storing up wealth to hand it over to the one that pleases God.... Eccles. 2:26 (NIV)

In other words, God has allowed sinners to start businesses, prove ideas, and prosper until His people rise and begin to use their like talents in the same fields. Once we employ our talents under God's direction, we will prosper even more greatly than the sinner. Because God is directing our businesses, customers will be drawn from everywhere, even away from the sinner. However, until we begin to move out in faith, God will allow the sinner to continue to supply the needs of the body.

We will find that the businesses that we start will be more than valuable, to the point of meeting basic needs and witnessing. Our efforts will bless others. We will administer life to others, which the sinner who does not know God is unable to do (II Cor. 9:10-15; I Pet. 4:10).

Being enriched in every thing to all bountifulness, which causeth through us thanksgiving to God. II Cor. 9:11

Because of our obedience to the Word of God, including maintaining a high quality standard in all our works, every thing we do will prosper.

This book of the law shall not depart out of thy mouth; but thou shalt meditate therein day and night, that thou mayest observe to do according to all that is written therein: for then thou shalt make thy way prosperous, and then thou shalt have good success. Josh. 1:8

The Proverbs 31 Woman Is Industrious

NOTES

Chapter 17

Faith

Verse 25

She is clothed in strength and dignity; she can laugh at the days to come. (NIV)

Strength and honor are her clothing; and she shall rejoice in time to come. (KJV)

Key Words

Strength	= vigor, energy, sturdiness
Dignity	= self-respect, character, distinction

As Christians, our hearts and minds should be continually fixed on God. We need to renew our minds, so that we can be transformed. It is through our reading of the Word and our intimate relationship with God that we come to know Him as all powerful, loving, and faithful.

It is because of our faith in God's word that we can walk confidently.

Just as praise is a garment that we put on to shield ourselves from and send away the demons that bring heaviness, becoming knowledgeable of God's word and receptive to the Holy Spirit will cause us to protect our bodies from the lies of the enemy.

It is through the knowledge of God's word that we clothe ourselves with strength and dignity. First, we know the authority we have in Christ to defeat the enemy in every matter (Matt. 16:18-19).

I will give you the keys of the kingdom of heaven; whatever you bind on earth will be bound in heaven and whatever you loose on earth will be loosed in heaven. Matt. 16:19 (NIV)

Second, we recognize that we are the sons and daughters of God and as such we are part of a royal priesthood.

But ye are a chosen generation, a royal priesthood, an holy nation, a peculiar people; that ye should shew forth the praises of Him who hath called you out of darkness into His marvellous light. I Pet. 2:9

Therefore we dress ourselves in dignity. Dignity of the saints is confidence in Christ and walking in righteousness. We know we are in His righteousness when we bear His fruit.

But the fruit of the Spirit is love, joy, peace, long-suffering, gentleness, goodness, faith,

Meekness, temperance: against such there is no law. Gal. 5:22-23

Now, it is because of our knowledge of both the spoken and written Word that we can laugh at the days to come. The closer we get to God, the more He will show us things in this time and times to come. So, no matter how satan manipulates our circumstances and no matter how many lies he tells us, we find ourselves laughing. We laugh because we see all the wonderful blessings God has prepared for us. We focus on what God shows us so much, that we hardly notice the shadows satan flashes around us.

We, as women of God, need to stay before the Lord for our families. We need to be stable in Him so that when they face trouble we can minister peace to them based on the knowledge God has shared with us. We don't focus on what we are going through, but we focus on what we are going to.

The Proverbs 31 Woman Is Steadfast and Unmovable

NOTES

Chapter 18

Stepping With the Holy Ghost

Verse 26

> *She speaks with wisdom, and faithful instruction is on her tongue.* (NIV)

> *She openeth her mouth with wisdom; and in her tongue is the law of kindness.* (KJV)

Key Words

Wisdom	=	spiritual insight from God
Law	=	precept, statute
Instruction	=	education, direction, teaching

Wisdom comes from God. It is through our communion with God that we gain wisdom over the knowledge of this world.

Behold, I stand at the door, and knock: if any man hear My voice, and open the door, I will come in to him, and will sup with him, and he with Me. Rev. 3:20

It is through the application of wisdom that we can overcome the world. But we must have a relationship to hear from God.

To him that overcometh will I grant to sit with me in My throne, even as I also overcame, and am set down with My Father in His throne.

He that hath an ear, let him hear what the Spirit saith unto the churches. Rev. 3:21-22

We women need to develop a personal relationship with God for ourselves, before we get involved in a marital relationship. It is through our relationship with God that He teaches us how to be in relationship with others. If we don't know how to submit ourselves to him we will not know how to submit effectively to other authorities in our lives, including our husbands.

Submission is an important principle. Outside submission to God we leave ourselves open to failure. For it is God that will direct us away from trouble.

Submit yourselves therefore to God. Resist the devil, and he will flee from you. James 4:7

Submission is the same as hiding yourself in God and taking refuge in him. We submit to Him because we trust or believe in Him. Therefore we wait for Him. We wait not for Him to "fix" things, but we wait to hear what He is saying to us about things. Then we put our hope in what He has said and we move according to His instruction (II Chron. 20:1-30).

And they rose early in the morning, and went forth into the wilderness of Tekoa: and as they went forth, Jehoshaphat stood and said, Hear me, O Judah, and ye inhabitants of Jerusalem; Believe in the Lord your God, so shall ye be established; believe His prophets, so shall ye prosper. II Chron. 20:20

Many people are going to miss their blessing because they refuse to trust God (Mark 5). Yes, we will receive whatever God has intended for us, but we must be in position to receive of Him.

We miss the blessings when, because of our lack of total submission, we move according to our own will (James 1:14-15).

But every man is tempted, when he is drawn away of his own lust, and enticed. James 1:14

So, when the blessings come knocking at the door, no one is home to answer. After receiving our blessings, we need to remain submitted to God because He will tell us how to keep them (Deut. 8).

Prayer Time

We must stay before God in prayer. The time we spend with Him is precious. It is God who will give us a response for all questions, including those concerning our families and our ministries.

Since we live by the Spirit, let us keep in step with the Spirit. Gal. 5:25 (NIV)

The Proverbs 31 Woman Is Led of the Spirit

NOTES

Chapter 19

Moving Forward

Verse 27

She watches over the affairs of her household and does not eat the bread of idleness. (NIV)

She looketh well to the ways of her household, and eateth not the bread of idleness. (KJV)

Key Words

Watch	= observe, contemplate, pay attention
Bread	= substance, livelihood
Idleness	= time-killing, inactivity, sluggishness

Again, God emphasizes this woman's diligence. She does not waste time by sitting before the television or in other idle activities. Instead, she spends time on things of value. She ensures that the home does not fall into disrepair and that someone pays the bills on time. Because of her diligence, God causes her to prosper in all things.

He who works his land will have abundant food, but he who chases fantasies lacks judgment. Prov. 12:11 (NIV)

God has a purpose for all things, including the hours of the day. If God did not intend for us to put each hour of the day to good use, including specified hours for sleeping, He would have made the day shorter. If there were not enough hours in a day to get our responsibilities done, He would have made the day longer.

Through submission to God and by the Spirit, He can direct our daily activities so that each day is productive and progressive. As we move forward by progression in God, we attain those things which God has prepared for us. That progression takes us to maturity in God.

The Proverbs 31 Woman Is Productive

NOTES

Chapter 20

Honor

Verse 28

Her children arise and call her blessed; her husband also, and he praises her. (NIV)

Her children arise up, and call her blessed; her husband also, and he praiseth her. (KJV)

Key Word

Arise	= grow up, mature, come into being

As her children mature and her family progresses, her family sees the light of God in her life. She is a beacon within her own home. As she and her husband walk uprightly before God, the blessings of the Lord overtake them.

Because she has sown to please the Spirit, her family highly esteems her. Her walk in the righteousness of Christ makes her a winner.

I believe all women with children want their children to think favorably of them or to believe that they are the best mothers in the world. Many women have tried various methods of winning this respect and esteem. Yet the scripture clearly shows us that these things come only through righteous living. By practicing and internalizing the word, we will walk in the righteousness of Christ.

Although children may not understand while they are young, as they mature they will come to honor and respect us for remaining steadfast in the things of God.

We cannot be women of compromise. Instead, we must strive to live up to the standards God has laid out for us (Phil. 3:12-14).

Not that I have already obtained all this, or have already been made perfect, but I press on to take hold of that for which Christ Jesus took hold of me. Phil. 3:12 (NIV)

When we do what the Word of God says, concerning our families, we gain their respect and honor.

The Proverbs 31 Woman Is Highly Esteemed

NOTES

Chapter 21

Right Relationship With God

Verse 29

Many women do noble things, but you surpass them all. (NIV)

Many daughters have done virtuously, but thou excellest them all. (KJV)

Key Words

Noble	= generous, magnificent, heroic
Surpass	= exceed, outdo, better

In the final synopsis, a man of God needs to walk with a true woman of God. One who submits to God and walks uprightly before Him. One who has such a relationship with God that she can pray and pray through to breakthrough. Because we have a strong relationship with God, our families and those we minister to value us highly.

Having a right relationship with God is more important than all the labors in the world (Luke 10:38-42).

But one thing is needful: and Mary hath chosen that good part, which shall not be taken away from her. Luke 10:42

All the characteristics we bear are rooted in our relationship with Him. Without it, our efforts will not stand up over time.

The Proverbs 31 Woman Is Reverent Unto God

NOTES

Chapter 22

Inner Over the Outer

Verse 30

Charm is deceptive, and beauty is fleeting; but a woman who fears the Lord is to be praised. (NIV)

Favor is deceitful, and beauty is vain: but a woman that feareth the Lord, she shall be praised. (KJV)

Key Words

Charm	=	grace, attractiveness
Deceptive	=	unreliable, misleading
Beauty	=	good looks, glamour
Fleeting	=	passing swiftly

Flesh lacks staying power, so do the works of the flesh. Yet obedience to God is most honorable. The woman who obeys God's commands should be honored and praised. Because of our faithfulness, God will make us the head and not the tail.

Many people evaluate others based solely on their outward appearance. The world has defined beauty by the outward features of a person. Many of us have bought into the world's philosophy of beauty, simply because we continuously learn it through the media. However, God places value on the condition of the heart which man cannot see with his natural eye.

Whose adorning let it not be that outward adorning of plaiting the hair, and of wearing of gold, or of putting on of apparel;

But let it be the hidden man of the heart, in that which is not corruptible, even the ornament of a meek and quiet spirit, which is in the sight of God of great price. I Pet. 3:3-4

Our flesh is constantly battling against our spirit and vying to take precedence over the spirit. Satan uses circumstances and the things of this world to distract us from what God has to say concerning us. Nevertheless, we have to remember that we are spirit clothed in flesh.

Flesh was created by that which is spirit. "Things" were birthed from the spirit. How then can the flesh be greater than the spirit that created it?

And fear not them which kill the body, but are not able to kill the soul: but rather fear him which is able to destroy both soul and body in hell. Matt. 10:28

So many of us have allowed the things of this world to dominate and control our spirits and our emotions. But as submitted women of God, we should live from the inside out not the outside in. Living by the spirit means our spirit is constantly in communication with the Spirit of God that gives us instruction.

We must base our efforts and actions upon what God has said. The body then is the vehicle used to carry out God's commands here on earth.

But we have this treasure in earthen vessels, that the excellency of the power may be of God, and not of us. II Cor. 4:7

Our focus should then be on building the spirit man and relationship with our God.

The Proverbs 31 Woman Is Inwardly Beautiful

NOTES

Chapter 23

Lasting Rewards

Verse 31

Give her the reward she has earned, and let her works bring her praise at the city gate. (NIV)

Give her of the fruit of her hands; and let her own works praise her in the gates. (KJV)

Key Words

Fruit	=	the result of a planted seed
Works	=	endeavors, efforts, accomplishments
Gate	=	a structure controlling passage through an opening

The Proverbs 31 woman receives eternal life after her journey. People remember her as a faithful and honorable woman, and God's glory has been revealed through her during her lifetime.

Sowing and reaping is a fundamental principle. As we sow to please the Spirit, from the Spirit we will receive eternal life.

For he that soweth to his flesh shall of the flesh reap corruption; but he that soweth to the Spirit shall of the Spirit reap life everlasting. Gal. 6:8

Because we persevere in the face of trial, we receive the crown of life.

Blessed is the man that endureth temptation: for when he is tried, he shall receive the crown of life, which the Lord hath promised to them that love Him. James 1:12

There is no way that we cannot be blessed if we follow righteousness. Blessings are the result of obedience to God's word. As I stated in the previous chapter, God will honor those who honor Him.

People will admire and respect us for remaining steadfast in the things of God. The works of our hands will bring forth lasting fruit. For that reason, people will praise God for enabling us to use our talents to serve others and advance the Kingdom of God.

The Proverbs 31 Woman Is an Overcomer and Receiver of Eternal Life

NOTES

Concluding Remarks

Proverbs 31 is a good starting place for women to begin their preparation for marriage and ministry. It shows us some characteristics of a royal woman of God. It also alludes to the character of a royal man of God.

We may not fully obtain all the characteristics laid out in these verses but we know the goal we are shooting for (Phil. 3:12-14).

I press toward the mark for the prize of the high calling of God in Christ Jesus. Phil. 3:14

Like all the Word, Proverbs 31 is laid out in perfect order and the analogies and symbols are perfect. Even the original audience of the passage is perfect. King Lemuel's mother is teaching him how to recognize a virtuous woman both before and after marriage. As part of a royal priesthood, we should seek to marry royal men and women of God.

As a single woman today, I intend to wait for the perfect-will mate that God has prepared (the prince). I would encourage all women to wait for God to bless them with the mate He has chosen for them. There can be nothing but joy and peace from waiting for and trusting God to bless.

The Proverbs 31 Woman Is...

Of Excellent Character
Trustworthy
Supportive
Honorable
Active in the Body of Christ
Informed
Responsible
A Good Steward
Capable
Faithful
Diligent
Compassionate
Wise
Regal
Submitted
Industrious
Steadfast
Unmovable
Led of the Spirit
Productive
Highly Esteemed
Reverent Unto God
Inwardly Beautiful
An Overcomer
A Receiver of Eternal Life